mac's year

1990

Cartoons from the Daily Mail

Stan McMurtry **mac**

Chapmans

Chapmans Publishers Ltd
141–143 Drury Lane
London WC2B 5TB

First published by Chapmans 1990

ISBN 1 85592 703 9

Printed and bound in Great Britain by
Clays Ltd, St Ives plc

A Devon man was unlucky enough to be the first person to be fined for breaking the now-customary summer hosepipe ban.

'Now we're in trouble! – it's one of those hosepipe detector units!' *August 24*

In an effort to control crime, Spanish police launched a huge summer crackdown against the Costa drugs trade.

'I was sitting on the beach unwrapping one of those little pills for holiday tummy, when all of a sudden . . .' *August 29*

A 69-year-old German teddy bear fetched £55,000 at auction in London. It had been valued at less than £1000.

'Oh, she's noticed, has she? Well, tell her daddy's taken them for nice walkies to Sotheby's.'

September 21

The EEC announced that it would take Britain to court over the country's polluted drinking water.

'I'm heartbroken not to be in Japan with you too, Maggie dear . . . yes dear, I'm being careful to avoid water with nitrates and lead in it . . .' *September 22*

Announcing its defence policy, the Green Party called it 'the hedgehog – you are just so prickly that no one would want to invade you.'

'Poor Sidney – he was just on his way to repel the Russian army menace for the Green Party.'
September 26

British Rail's bosses were given large pay rises – but their customers felt they had been given the bird.

'My goodness, Hodson. It's a relief not to have to travel on those filthy, overcrowded trains any more'

September 29

A row broke out after the Archbishop of Canterbury said that the government lacked compassion.

'Hey, Luigi, look – more friends of de Archbishop over froma England!' *October 2*

As Mikhail Gorbachev flew into East Germany, thousands of
its citizens were fleeing to freedom in the West.

'Surely everybody can't have left?' *October 6*

On the eve of the Tory Party conference, home loans looked set to rise to their highest level in seven years.

'It's not so much terrorists we're worried about this year, Nigel. It's people with mortgages.' *October 9*

The Soviet news agency Tass said that an alien spaceship manned by giant people with tiny heads had landed south-east of Moscow.

'Mr President! I have bad news concerning the Soviet–American space race. . . .' *October 12*

'Good grief, man! Don't you know the world's stockbrokers are facing extinction?' *October 16*

A fall on the New York stock market prompted fears of another crash in share values. Chancellor Nigel Lawson was not amused.

'Don't worry, they're doing old Harold Lloyd stunts – yesterday they had a bloke dangling from a clock.' *October 17*

'Thank heavens Britain doesn't sentence people to death like we do' *October 19*

Britain's roads continued to clog up. Still, traffic jams do at least encourage the art of conversation . . .

'. . . . and apparently they've got a car that does from nought to sixty in 5.8 seconds!' *October 20*

Both the police and the army were called in during the ambulancemen's strike.

'Apparently while you were semi-conscious after your car accident you signed some sort of confession' *October 23*

The annual Commonwealth Conference attracted the usual difference over South Africa and civil rights among member states.

'Right – is there any other business?' *October 24*

'Because nasty Mr Lawson has frozen child benefits. That's why you're rationed to six helpings of
Ambrosia of avocado and strawberry flambé . . .' *October 26*

Chancellor Nigel Lawson's resignation on 26 October sparked a crisis in the Tory ranks. Or did it? Not everyone seemed to think so.

'Drinks all round again? – That's very kind of you Mr Heath, Sir.' *October 30*

An ultra-sonic binocular-gun was 'the perfect way of nobbling race horses', a court was told.

'Of course they're just ordinary binoculars sir, but could we have a look?' *November 2*

Nigel Lawson's interview on television after his resignation
evidently did not go down too well in some quarters.

'Dammit, Maggie! I was going to watch golf after the Lawson interview! *November 6*

MPs were accused of double standards after awarding themselves an inflation-busting 10 per cent pay rise while holding out against the ambulancemen.

'Go steady on the celebrations, Percy old boy – you're making a speech savaging those greedy ambulancemen this afternoon.' *November 7*

As the ambulancemen's dispute hotted up in the winter of 1989,
Army Land Rovers were ordered in to fill the gap.

'You 'orrible man! You didn't think we'd rush you into intensive care with hair that length, did you?'
November 10

In London, twenty-five nuns organized a sponsored snooker tournament in order to raise money for their convent.

'Aw, c'mon, Sister Agatha! Stop messing about, play fair!' *November 16*

Michael Heseltine's denials that he wanted Margaret Thatcher's
job drew a sceptical response from some quarters.

'Psst! Maggie Dear. Did you give Heseltine permission to measure the curtains and carpets?'
November 20

The controversial decision to televise the House of Commons became a reality on 21 November 1989 when the cameras were switched on for the first time.

'Actually he's out with his secretary again – this is in case his wife is watching TV' *November 23*

Nerves began to fray in the Tory Party during the run up to Sir Anthony Meyer's challenge to Margaret Thatcher's leadership on 5 December 1989.

'I'm sorry, the Prime Minister is in America right now. This is her husband – No, she's not worried by any leadership challenge.' *November 24*

Rumania proved to be the last – and the bloodiest – tyranny to fall in Eastern Europe.

'AAAH FREEDOM!' *November 27*

Lady Diana Mosley, the widow of fascist leader Sir Oswald Mosley, was an unexpected choice of guest on *Desert Island Discs*.

'Look up a minute, Adolf, it's Desert Island Discs! Oswald Mosley's wife says you've got mesmeric blue eyes . . .' *November 28*

The government's refusal to increase war widows' pensions provoked a national outcry. Eventually, the government relented.

'. . . and so, the world waits and hopes that the East German people may soon have economic freedom and all the prosperity it brings. . . .' *November 30*

The plight of the Vietnamese Boat People in Hong Kong provoked a sharp difference of opinion between the British and US governments.

'She's heartless! We've killed half their relatives, bombed, defoliated and napalmed their country. How could Maggie send them back to that dump?' *December 1*

High winds and rough seas disrupted the winter summit between George Bush and Mikhail Gorbachev on board ship off Malta.

'The first topic to come up was arms control, then Europe came up, then breakfast, then lunch, then . . .' *December 4*

A love mystery deepened after it was alleged that Rumanian gymnast Nadia Comaneci planned to marry a man who already had a wife and four young children.

'Honestly darling! Nothing has happened between us – Nadia's never still long enough!' *December 5*

Dodgy electrical goods or dodgy loyalty among MPs? The Prime Minister's popularity slumped at the end of 1989.

'Just a few Christmas presents for some colleagues – I'd like sixty highly dangerous microwave ovens, gift wrapped . . .' *December 7*

As the Berlin Wall was pulled down, a nebulous trade in 'souvenirs' soon arose.

'You're right, Hamish. A piece of the Berlin Wall is a politically significant symbol of the 1980s and a wonderful gift, but I still think your relatives will recognise our old outside loo.' *December 11*

America's hard-line stand on the Vietnamese Boat People drew
strong criticism from some quarters.

'Of course, we must do everything we can to help those poor, poor Germans. . . .' *December 12*

The government announced plans to prosecute alleged Nazi war criminals living in Britain. But who and where were they?

'We haf ways of making you talk!' *December 14*

'I heard that Kylie often wished she was a checkout girl – so we swapped.' *December 15*

On 17 December, hurricane-force winds and torrential storms
left a trail of destruction across Britain.

'Wonderful news, dear — my water share certificates have arrived!' *December 18*

A Commons Select Committee said that 'the accommodation of even several millions from Hong Kong would be quite possible if shared among the international community'.

'Surely there must be some other way you could have set an example?' *December 19*

Speaking at a prize-giving, Prince Charles said that the Church of England was at the heart of the 'calamitous decline' of the English language.

'Is that the dismal wasteland of the English language Prince Charles was talking about, Miss Pringle?'

December 21

Britain's top earners looked set for massive pay rises – while the ambulancemen remained on strike.

'I see, how terribly interesting – so if one's massive pay claim is refused one simply holds out one's bucket and the public put money into it.' *January 15*

Princess Anne's call for people to behave more responsibly struck a chord. But has Cruncher even passed his driving test?

'Admit it, Cruncher – your Mum's been listening to Princess Anne again, ain't she?' *January 18*

Storm in a sporran: One of Scotland's senior judges resigned amid allegations that some judges were gay.

'Och it canna be! That long hair, those flowing red robes! I thought his name was Gertrude!' *January 19*

Maverick judge James Pickles was branded 'an ancient dinosaur' after gaoling a teenage mother whose three-month-old baby would have to go to prison with her. She appealed.

'Cellmate for you, Mangler – straight from Judge Pickles's court. Don't forget to change his nappy.'
January 22

Tough action against noise vandals was promised by the government. Offenders could assuredly expect a midnight knock.

'We've had a complaint from next door about your husband's snoring.' *January 23*

Calls for more women in Britain's boardrooms drew a muted
response – from men.

'You see, this is why you'll never make management Mrs Winthorp – you move your head and don't
follow through . . .' *January 25*

Margaret Thatcher decided to scrap plans to make football fans carry identity cards to matches. But the problem of how to control thuggery remained.

'I think I preferred the identity cards idea – at least there was a chance of slipping through the turnstiles.' *January 29*

The flowering of democracy in Eastern Europe prompted talk of a 'peace dividend' and the return of US forces to America.

'DAMN!' *January 30*

'When you said you were in newspapers and could take me to Tramp, this isn't what I had in mind!'
February 1

Huge crowds turned out for the opening of Moscow's – and
Russia's – first MacDonald's burger bar.

'Now he's allowed in McDonald's and Big Macs, I wonder what this exciting new idea is he's got for
Red Square?' *February 2*

As services on the East Anglia route to London came in for criticism, British Rail announced swingeing fare increases.

'I told you this would happen if they kept putting the fares up!' *February 6*

In an attempt to reduce the population of Britain's crumbling prisons, the Home Secretary encouraged the courts not to send minor offenders to gaol.

'Oh stop moaning, Sidney! At least you're at home and not in one of those overcrowded prisons.'

February 8

Following his resignation from the government, Nigel Lawson secured a job at Barclay's Bank with a six-figure salary.

'Comrade President, do we need a part-time economic adviser? – only £200,000 a year plus luncheon vouchers.' *February 9*

After twenty-seven years in prison, Nelson Mandela walked to
freedom on 11 February 1990.

'After 27 years it's lovely having a man about the house again, Nelson.' *February 13*

The long-awaited Guinness trial has just begun, with leading financiers in the dock on a raft of criminal charges.

'Sorry darling. It's jusht my bad luck. Thish trial could last for weeksh. . . .' *February 15*

As interest rates soared, Perrier withdrew its bottled mineral water after a pollution scare at the factory.

'I'm worried. Donald is taking it pretty badly.' *February 16*

'I'm from "Eurotunnel" in England, Mrs Trump – will you marry me?' *February 19*

Margaret Thatcher risked international criticism when she warned of the dangers of a headlong rush to German reunification.

'Don't you think you're being just a shade over-pessimistic about German reunification, Maggie dear?'

February 20

The White House announced a plan to drop millions of caterpillars into the South American jungles to eat the cocaine crop before the plants could be processed.

'Of course, Mr President, over in Bolivia they'll have the cocaine crops to concentrate on. . . .'
February 22

An ageing horse saddled its owner with a £50 fine – for speeding
in Richmond Park. The owner appealed.

'Speeding fine or not,' I said, 'no jumped-up little policeman is going to stop me galloping my horse in the park!' *February 23*

'Patience, comrades! We're doing our best to speed up the path to Western-style democracy . . .'
February 26

Floods, storms and winds of 100 m.p.h. battered the country. Weathermen said they had no idea why Britain was getting such a pounding from gales.

'Relax darling, panic's over. I've managed to get through to the emergency services. They're coming to fix the TV.' *February 27*

The Advertising Standards Authority warned that it would start to get tough with companies that used sex to sell their products.

'Remember, now, Doris. When the man from the flat below asks to borrow some coffee – no smouldering looks!' *March 1*

Olympic javelin champion Tessa Sanderson won £30,000 in libel damages from Robert Maxwell's Mirror Group. And the answer to the question is yes.

'That reminds me, Mr Maxwell, Sir. Have we sent Tessa Sanderson her £30,000 yet?' *March 2*

Britain's reputation as the 'dirty man of Europe' led to promises of tough action from the government – for everyone.

'That's Louie – he did a "whoopsie" in the sea at Great Yarmouth.' *March 5*

Allegations surfaced that Arthur Scargill's NUM had received cash from Colonel Qadaffi during the miner's strike. Arthur threatened legal action.

'Can I take it you won't be helping Arthur with any legal fees then, Colonel?' *March 6*

'As you'll be occupying this cell for quite a while I'm afraid you're liable for poll tax. . . .' *March 8*

A Department of Trade Report was critical of the Fayed
brothers during the take-over battle for Harrods.

'There's a rumour going around that you borrowed the money for the takeover from Arthur Scargill.'
March 9

'**Denis! You forgot the secret knock – there's 30,000 volts going through that door knob.**' *March 12*

While Mikhail Gorbachev won supreme power as President of the Soviet Union, hysterical talk among Tory MPs threatened Mrs Thatcher's standing.

'It's Mrs Thatcher, President Gorbachev sir – have you got any helpful tips?' *March 13*

In his Budget, Chancellor John Major increased the price of a pint – and incentives to save.

'Aw, please folks! Come over and have a drink.' *March 21*

The Great Poll Tax Blunder: After the Chancellor said that
Scots tax payers would not qualify for relief, Mrs Thatcher
quickly stepped in with a £4 million subsidy.

'You know, Angus, Hamish here may be right. £4 million isn't too bad considering none of us has been
paying the Poll Tax anyway.' *March 23*

'If by some remote chance you did get ousted in a leadership bid, Maggie dear – any plans?' *March 26*

Film star Glenda Jackson was selected to fight the next election as the Labour candidate for Hampstead and Highgate in north London.

'I trust that seeing the new Labour candidate for Hampstead in action hasn't changed the voting habits of a lifetime, Gerald?' *March 29*

'I'm sorry, President Hussein. You just can't get the parts nowadays!' *March 30*

Poll tax protestors went on the rampage in Central London,
causing thousands of pounds of damage.

April 2

Immigration rebel Norman Tebbit and his supporters were
unhappy at the prospect of 225,000 Hong Kong Chinese coming
to Britain.

'Personally I agree with Tebbit – our little country is overcrowded enough as it is . . .' *April 6*

The prison siege at Strangeways monopolised April headlines.

'Year after year a prisoner in the kitchen, trapped by domesticity and housework, I suddenly had an urge to climb on the roof and throw tiles ...' *April 9*

Saudi Arabia tops the list of earnings for employees of British firms overseas, according to a new survey. A junior executive in Riyadh nearly doubles his UK spending power.

'I'm sure some expatriates do earn lots more money in Saudi Arabia but let's face it, there doesn't seem to be much call for encyclopaedias . . .' *April 12*

British Customs agents netted the world's biggest gun on board
a ship bound for Iraq. The Iraqis maintained that the 'super gun'
was an oil pipeline.

'When you arrive in Iraq captain, would you mind handing President Hussein this bill for evading
customs duty?' *April 13*

With Neil Kinnock in the VIP box, there was a huge concert at Wembley Stadium to honour Nelson Mandela. George Michael and Stevie Wonder topped the bill.

'What am I thinking about, Winnie? I'm thinking about my nice quiet cell in South Africa, that's what I'm thinking about . . .' *April 17*

Critics blamed left-wing teachers for the problems in Britain's schools.

'Sent to our bedroom without any tea again! I'm sure Militant has infiltrated his nursery school.'

April 19

'Hello, Mr Ridley? Look, we're getting a teensy weensy bit uneasy about these decorative doorstops we're making for Iraq . . .' *April 20*

As always, the London Marathon in April sorted the men from the boys – or girls.

'Have you no compassion, woman? I've sat through hours of gruelling snooker without a cup of tea!'

April 23

The government's plans to regulate human embryo research
had all-party support – or did they?

'We've kept to your instructions, Prime Minister – that one's going to be a Labour supporter . . .'
April 24

Riot or farce? The trouble at Strangeways prison in Manchester
dominated the nation's TV screens. The authorities stood by.

'Dammit! We should have known this would happen. Who let those builders climb up there?' *April 26*

During a month of prison riots, Labour announced its alternative to the Tory poll tax.

'Now let's get this straight. You say you stripped the prison roof to save us having to pay the Labour party's roof tax?' *April 27*

'Dry, sunny and warm weather is in store for most of the week,'
Ian McCaskill predicted. Meanwhile Tories desperately rallied
support for the coming local government elections.

**'Remember folks, this absolutely free, glorious spell of hot weather is brought to you by courtesy of
the Conservative party . . .'** *April 30*

Amid considerable debate, the government suggested plans to
introduce a registration scheme for the nation's dogs.

'I had a feeling this would happen once we became registered.' *May 1*

Sweeping Labour gains were predicted in the 3 May local council elections. The Tories tried to reason why.

'Golly! – Cigars, a lift to the polling station and champagne afterwards! – Who's paying for all this?'

May 3

A national newspaper published a 'damning dossier' on drink and drugs parties in a Midlands prison. Staff at another prison said that the high jinks were a nightly occurrence.

'Poor old Chalky – he's going home tomorrow.' *May 4*

A blunder by football chiefs was blamed for a weekend of
seaside rioting after the Leeds–Bournemouth game drew louts
from all over the country.

'Really? Three Leeds football fans? You spoil that rottweiler, Mr Harrigan.' *May 7*

The Prince and Princess of Wales visited Hungary, although it was suspected that the Prince had not packed his paintbox.

'For Heaven's sake, Ludmilla! He hasn't got his art materials with him!' *May 8*

A Japanese traffic researcher claimed that a motorist's star sign radically affected his or her behaviour at the wheel. Capricorns, he said, were the worst of all.

'Hello, hello, hello, Capricorns are likely to meet a man dressed in red wearing a wig, I see a small room with bars at the window . . .' *May 11*

'It's not as bad as I feared – she's only got "extremely silly cow disease."' *May 15*

Prince Charles said that society neglected the skills and talents of the elderly. And their pulling power?

'Psst lucky girls! Do you realise you're sitting beside a wealth of talent waiting to be tapped?' *May 17*

'Good evening. Tonight I can report wonderful news for the Tories. An opinion poll has shown massive support for . . . AAAAAAAGH!' *May 18*

Couturier Sir Hardy Amies revealed that Her Majesty has a
keen eye for a bargain.

'Oh dear, I hope she's not going to keep moaning about the prices again.' *May 22*

Tracy Edwards and *Maiden* near the end of the Whitbread round-the-world race. The crew were all girls.

'Sorry about this lads but we're within sight of Southampton.' *May 24*

Labour launched a new manifesto as 'mad cow' fever gripped the country. The Tories hoisted a red peril warning.

Believe me folks. There's no scientific proof that 'mad Kinnock disease' can hurt human beings . . .

May 25

The EEC condemned ninety-seven beaches in England and
Wales for their high pollution levels.

'Tell us about the Dunkirk beaches, Grandad – were they as bad as Blackpool?' *May 28*

A jubilant Tracy Edwards, skipper of the all-girl yacht *Maiden*, stepped ashore at the end of the 33,000-mile Whitbread round-the-world race.

'Mother. If you're thinking what I think you're thinking, – we haven't got a compass, a map or any sandwiches!' *May 29*

On a visit to Washington, Mikhail Gorbachev learned that his arch-rival, Boris Yeltsin, had become President of the Russian Federation.

'Aw, c'mon Mikhail! Forget Yeltsin for a while and join the banquet. Barbara went to a lot of trouble.'
May 31

Agriculture Minister John Gummer discounted scares over BSE – and had his daughter sample a hamburger in front of the cameras.

'Don't worry m'sieu. This lot are fully guaranteed. Each cow has been bitten personally by John Gummer's daughter.' *June 1*

Tough police tactics against rowdies at the World Cup in
Sardinia drew criticism from English fans – but not, it is
thought, from the long-suffering locals.

'I don't care what Colin Moynihan says – I still think you Italian police are over-reacting!' *June 18*

Two suspected IRA terrorists cornered in a Belgian wood claimed that they were innocent sweethearts on a pre-wedding holiday. Police promptly arrested them.

'Don't move, you're surrounded – Anti-Terrorist Squad!' *June 19*

Fashionable Royal Ascot opened to a parade of bizarre, batty and brilliant hats. One lady wore a home-made cheeseburger on her head . . .

'It allows me to indulge in champagne and caviar and salve my social conscience at the same time, my dear.' *June 21*

Chancellor John Major floated a proposal for a new Euro-currency, the 'hard ECU'. Many people thought the idea could ECU-off.

'Oh, touring Europe, sir? Our Mr Brinkley at the end desk will be glad to convert it into Ecus for you.'

June 22

For a few heady days, World Cup fever met Wimbledon frenzy.
The domestic consequences promised to be dire . . .

'Me too. A slight marital tiff over whether to watch the World Cup or Wimbledon . . .' *June 25*

Two passenger jets came within seconds of a mid-air collision while flying at 500 m.p.h. at 28,000 feet over Wales.

'Nice to see they're doing something positive at last about all these near misses . . .' *June 26*

'Poor devil! I think it's the producer of that London West End show Bernadette.' *June 28*

Tennis officials suspected that the Mafia had moved in on Wimbledon's million-pound ticket touting trade. Outside the ground, touts described the claims as 'outrageous'.

'I don't care how much you paid for it, that seat's taken!' *June 29*

'You're free to go now – be thankful it was only a broken arm!' *July 2*

East finally went West when East Germany dropped its own currency and adopted the West German deutschmark. Would that life was so simple for Mikhail Gorbachev.

'Lunchbreak at last. Nip over to East Germany and buy a few sandwiches lad . . .' *July 3*

England met West Germany in the World Cup and kept the entire nation (or at least one half of it) glued to the television all evening.

'All right Girls, we can go home now – there goes the "all-clear".' *July 5*

British Rail's annual report admitted that trains were later and
carriages dirtier. Meanwhile fares continued to rise.

'You're late, filthy and covered in rat bites again, Simpson! – why don't you travel by road?' *July 6*

Despite the support of NUM loyalists, Arthur Scargill became embroiled in allegations concerning miners' money in European bank accounts.

'I hope you're not forced to pay a £15 registration fee for every one of your LAP DOGS, Arthur . . .'
July 10

Betting on the 'Archbishop Stakes' – the choice of a successor to Dr Runcie – hotted up when a bookmaker declared that 'our turnover is already double what we anticipated'.

'And now brethren, a short prayer for the elevation of the Reverend David Sheppard who at 5–1 could earn me 500 smackers at Ladbrokes . . .' *July 12*

Ice queen Jayne Torvill revealed that although she was still arm in arm with partner Christopher Dean, her heart had gone to another. She had been secretly engaged for three months.

'He's not going to start getting all possessive, is he, Jayne?' *July 13*

In the wake of the Ridley Affair a leaked government minute contained an assessment of the German character which included 'angst, aggressiveness, bullying, egotism, inferiority complex and sentimentality'.

'No, no, Denis! We finished the German characteristics assessment seminar last week. Please get changed . . .' *July 16*

'Typical of that woman, Mr President. Making those ridiculous assessments of German characteristics
– what other nation would stoop so low?' *July 17*

In Britain for a concert, superstar Madonna decided to take a morning jog through Hyde Park accompanied by a posse of minders.

'Now's your chance, Bernard – nip down the manhole and get Madonna's autograph . . .' *July 20*

On 22 July, Nick Faldo won the British Open Golf
Championship. On 23 July, Margaret Thatcher finalized her
summer reshuffle . . .

'I see she's started on her reshuffle . . .' *July 23*

The authorities banned a Moslem film showing *Satanic Verses* author Salman Rushdie shooting and abusing Moslems before being struck dead by a bolt of lightning. It was later released on video.

'Excuse me – could you spare a little tomato ketchup?' *July 24*

'This fellow who's offered to handle the new royal finances – does his face seem familiar to you?'
July 26

Aliens? Hoaxers? Nutty scientists? The crop circles in the West
Country provided fun for all.

'Haven't you got anywhere else but Wiltshire?' *July 27*